Whispers of the New Earth

Title: Whispers of the New Earth: Energetic Inspiration for Light Beings, Starseeds, Rainbow Warriors, Unicorns and Fairies
Author: Janneke Hellebrekers
Cover Art: Seerendip Publishing
Publisher: Seerendip Publishing
Edition: First printing, 2024
ISBN: 978-1-965273-06-7 (Paperback)
Printed in the United States of America

Thank you to all who were with me on my journey. Especially to my loving supportive partner Hydro, our lovely families by blood and soul, and all my wonderful sisters.

The tears, the laughter, the ups and downs were all worth it and I could not have done it without you.

Welcome lovely beings!

Thank you for being here on earth.

It's an honor to be here with you.

From here it can only get onwards and upwards to more and more exciting times ahead.

First, you needed to see it to believe it, then you needed to believe it to see it and now you just know it.
We entered the age of knowing.

You can use any page as an oracle to ask questions and see what answers come to you.
Or use my writing as affirmations and activations that you can repeat as much as you want.

See and feel the words vibrating through you.

May these words uplift you when you forget where you came from and may they inspire you on your journey.

Lots of love!

Hey there magnificent light being!
Yes, you give light in the dark even if you are
unaware of it; how cool is that!

You are a human glow stick.
You are amazing.
You are a visionary.
You are the new energy.
You are the new earth.

You are energy in motion.
Let your emotions go
and you will flow.

Conscious warriors, conscious resistance.
Going with the flow of life itself.
We are the pioneers of the new earth.
The leaders of the vision for the future.

The fear is just nonsense.
Let's all just be brave.

Letting the story be the story.
Owning your story,
but don't let it define you.

I AM a soldier of God's army.
Nothing can stop me.
I AM free.
And I know it.

Reality gets more and more amazing,
but also more weird and surreal.
Enjoy the ride!

We are an ancient species of superconscious beings.
Incarnated to uplift and assist humanity with the great
awakening.

Activate your light body and recreate your whole
existence.
We have a whole universe inside of us.

I am an angel stuck in density.
I come from higher realms bringing in more light
and love to this world
and I will return back to these realms.

There is no dark and light.
Everything is sound and vibration.
There is no separation.
We dwell in the middle.
Where everything is god.

Every day you have the choice to reinvent yourself.
Who do you want to be?
Make more conscious choices.
Fear or love, the choice is yours.

Every time you heal, you and your reality becomes lighter and brighter.
So if we all do this, reality gets better for everyone.

Why do we cling onto our pain?
Why is it more difficult to be present with our pain than with our pleasure?
The more we can feel the pain, the more we can feel the pleasure and really be present with it.

If the choice is not fully there yet,
its because something else that is more epic is on its way.

Trust
There is wisdom in the universe.
There is a thread even though you don't know the whole road yet.
Keep putting one foot after the other. You can do it.
Keep going.
You are loved and taken care of.

I am here to create magic on earth.
And to remind you of its magic.

The more you focus on the reality you want, the more
reality will bring that back to you.

You can tap into what you want to feel by saying the
words you want to experience.
For instance:
Love and Abundance.
Joy and Excitement.
Peace and Tranquility.
Harmony and balance.
You can feel it while you say it and the more you say it,
the more you bring it in.

To be connected with yourself and your heart does not
cost any energy.
Worrying costs energy.
Not being yourself costs energy.
Just be you and enjoy

and everything will fall into place.
Relax in this moment.

Singing and humming brings you out of your head and
into the present moment.

I really like my reality and it gets better and better.

Fill yourself up with light and be a light for others.

Perfectionism can be a good thing,
because you know what you want,
but let go of the high expectations and beating yourself
up when things don't go as expected.
Know that everything has a reason, even every so-called
mistake.

There are no mistakes.
Know everything will make sense at one point.
Only you never know when that time comes.

Just trust it will all be there in divine timing.
Have patience.

Feel the excitement
that our galactic brothers and sisters may come.
………..
And if not, just feel the excitement anyway.

Be the love you missed growing up,
be your own father and mother.
You are the one you are waiting for.

I want to remind you that you are that light.
Your light lights up the world around you.
You may not always experience it, but know you are.

When you find it inside, no one needs to confirm it to you,
and you just radiate it out into the world.

Reminder:
You are not responsible for the happiness of
everyone,
but you are fully responsible for your own happiness.

You have days you feel really strange or sad,
but fortunately, you have more days that you feel amazing
and life is wonderful.
You just keep riding the waves.

Please don't make up a story in your head about me,
Because you have no idea who I am.
I am still figuring myself out.

See the signs,
They are everywhere.

I surrender to who I am in any moment.

When are you going to love yourself enough
to not harm yourself anymore?

You can have a new start every day.
You deserve all the best to help you become your greatest,
grandest version.
You can start any moment.
Step by step will get you there.
No need to know the whole story yet.

The world needs your open heart.
The world needs your medicine.

The universe shows me over and over again
that it is kind, loving, and full of awesome
surprises.

Let every day bring its magic to you.

I am whole.
You are whole.
The only one who thinks (s)he is not whole is a creation
of the mind.

Don't let it play tricks on you.
You are stronger and bigger than that.

No need to fear.
No need to worry.
You are carried by the universe.

There is always space for more gratitude.

Start to feel already abundant
and you will manifest it even quicker.

Don't ever forget to keep dancing through life, whatever
music is played.
And know you can change the music as well.

I am not here to create followers.
I am here to create leaders.
Once you wake up to your empowered self. You don't
need anyone telling you how to live.

The rebellion gives you the fire to do what you need to do.
The anger towards the system was necessary to break free from it.

The only suffering is the rejection of the present moment.
Change what you can, accept the rest and you are free.

Life is amazing and you are as well.
Life is a gift and you are as well.

The more you show up as your full self.
The more responsibility you have.
The more rewards come to you.
The more love you give out,
The more love you get back.

Life is happening wherever I AM.

Love is here.
And love has won.
And it keeps on winning.

Soultribe
We vibe because we are from the same tribe.
Forever growing in our knowing.
And rising in love and light.
Forever getting more bright.
Becoming our greater version every day.
And ready for all the good things coming our way.

The universe will keep showering you with many
blessings.

The sky is the limit
of what you can achieve and receive.

We are working on another blueprint for Mother Earth
to live a life in love, beauty, and harmony together as one.

Living a life in abundance and going into transcendence to higher realms of awesomeness.

You are here to experience the fullness that is life and that is you.

Be all you can be and shine bright as the sun.
As you allow yourself to shine,
you inspire others to shine as well.

Awakening is an ongoing journey of discovering all that you can be
and even more in every moment.

You got this!
You will overcome this.
You are amazing.
And you are doing great.
I love you.

I see you.
I admire your strength and your dedication. Everything will be ok.
Just have a bit more patience and trust everything will work out.

If other people don't see how awesome you are it's no problem,
as long as you know you are.

For eyes that see.
Ears that hear.
Skin that feels.
Everything is already here.

Life is to be expressed, enjoyed, experienced, and loved.
No need to understand.
Live it like the unique expression that is you.

Everything is perfect, just as it is.

You are here to light up this world
with your kindness.
Your compassion.
Your smile.
Your hugs.
Your truth.
Your wisdom.
Most of all let your love be expressed however you want
to express it in the moment.

I may not be perfect,
but every day I strive to be the best possible human that I
know.
To be kind, honest, responsible, loving, happy, smiley, and
to be there for myself and other beings.
To love myself and others
every day a bit more.
To feel more freedom, truth, and love within myself more
and more each day.

I always do my best, but I also know I can do better in every next moment.

We are here to enjoy the f#ck out of this reality.
Sometimes we forget and then we come back to it over and over again.

Be easy on each other.
Everybody has such a different parallel reality. Everybody is a whole unique universe on their own.

You are on the right path, don't despair.
Everything will work out.

Just relax and breathe.
Always expect wonderful things to happen. Anything can happen,
anythings happen all the time.
There is a fine line between going after things and taking action
or relaxing and letting things come to you.

Trust that all the answers always come to you in the right divine time.

Before getting a clear yes you need to experience some doubts.
It is all necessary to make even better decisions.

How can you be anything less than perfect? How can everything you do be anything less than perfect?

There is sooooo much magic in the universe.
See it and feel it.
Just have faith and trust that everything perfectly evolves as it needs to.
More love.
More fun.
More Joy.
More happiness.
More fulfillment.
More abundance.

More radiance.
More understanding.
More play.
More bliss.

When you don't care what other people think of you, you
are truly free.
When you limit yourself out of fear, that means you put
their importance higher than yours.
You are more important than anybody else.

When one door closes,
trust that life has other plans.
And know there are still infinite other doors waiting for
you.

We came here to rock this reality.
And participate in the biggest celebration the universe
has ever known.

I am more and more myself every day.
How liberating is that?

Focus on what makes you happy and more things will
come on your path that will.
Even if you feel you are not there yet,
It is ok.
Life gets better and better each day.

Keep being sane in this insane reality.
It is not you, but this world.
But by changing you, you change the world.

If the path is not clear yet, don't move.

I AM all that I AM.
I AM great.
I AM abundant.
I AM awesome.
I AM loving.
I AM love.

Every day when you wake up.
Ask how you can serve the earth and humanity.
While having more love, freedom, and joy.

It takes courage and strength to make different choices
and to take the road less traveled.
You can be proud of your bravery.

I AM grateful for my life and everyone in it.
Life can be amazing if you allow it to be.

Every day I get an opportunity to show up more.
Be more present.
Be more myself.
Be more courageous.

Grateful to be more me every day.

I choose to be joyful and enthusiastic.

I believe it is possible, do you??

Joy

Celebrate and have fun.

Joy and ecstasy flow through me wildly and freely.

Freedom

Break free.

Express yourself.

And let your spirit free.

Boundless freedom surges through me.

I listen to my heart and follow its guidance.

I deserve to be happy.

I have the power to create my reality.

I trust that all will work out well.

My life is clear of blocks.

I love and accept all that I AM.

There is nothing to change,

there is only love.

Every aspect in me serves both me and the whole.

I create balance and harmony by loving what is.
I know that love transforms into even greater love.

I AM the light that lights up this world.
My light radiates through me to the world around me.

I love myself and my life.
I love the people in my life.
And I AM grateful for the life I am living.
I learn every day.
I grow every day.
There is infinite expansion.

Why can't we all just be more kind to each other? If we are not kind to ourselves in our thoughts, words, and actions, how can we expect to be kind to others?
Start being more kind to yourself and see your life transform.

I AM open to receiving all the gifts of the universe.

I let go of all contracts or limitations in all dimensions, timelines, and space and so it is.

Life surprises me with more amazingness!

All realizations are self-realizations.
Everything is one big mirror.

Often what you don't like in another,
you don't like within yourself.
Especially the behaviors you see in your parents.
The more you can accept them as they are, The more you can accept yourself as you are.

Embrace the void and the unexpected,
Maybe it is even better than you ever expected.

You are a magnificent creature of light.

We are strong.
We are free.
We are one humanity!

Life is amazing and ever unfolding.
Even if you don't know where it is going,
know it will be amazing because you are.

You can do anything you want.
And live the life of your dreams.
We are here on earth not to survive,
but to thrive on all levels.
You have this power within and you will connect to
this once the chatter of the outside world becomes more
silent.
Then you start listening to your intuition and your heart.
And you start using your mind as your servant to make it
all happen.
Know there are infinite possibilities to choose from. The
more you follow your heart,
the better the choices and your life will be.

You do you!

Whatever it is, that makes you feel you again, do that!
You don't have to travel anywhere in the world, to find
new hidden depths within your soul.

We deserve to live in a world where every human being
has everything they want.
We all deserve it and there is enough for all.
This universe is abundant,
you are abundant.

There are always more layers to let go of.
Shedding off all the skin that is not you anymore. So you
become more and more you every day.

Go and do what sets your soul on fire.
The universe is giving you hunches all the time. You just
need to keep showing up.
To the cosmic party that is made especially for you.

I give love freely and abundantly to myself and others.

By giving to others, I receive it as well.

So grateful to be the conduit to share the love that is there for all of us.

Be free to be you.
Feel free to express your unique being.

I deserve peace, abundance, and love.
And I create it myself in co-creation with the universe.

There is always room for becoming a better version of yourself,
but already love yourself where you are now. Unleash your gifts into the universe.
You are born for this time to show up.

No more fear.
No more hiding.
No more playing small.

You are here to do amazing things.

Let me be a beacon of light and love
and let me inspire others to remember they are that as
well.

I don't want to fit in.
I just want to be me.
It's okay to be me.

More and more inspiration is coming into my life every day.
And more realizations that bring more truth and wisdom.

I open myself to divine source flowing through me, and it
feels good.

I can do what I want.
I can say what I want.
I can feel what I want.
I can create what I want.

I see the beauty and the potential in people.
Even when they don't see it themself
and I will remind them of it.

Talk to yourself as if you are your own biggest fan.

The more I love and accept others as they are, the more I
love and accept myself as I am.

You are welcome as you are at this moment. Feel safe to
be you.
There is no need to prove anything to anyone.

Can you feel the love and light that you are? Can you see
and feel it reflected back by life and the people around
you?
How can you give that even more to yourself and others?
The more you give, the more you receive.

You are that sun that shines on everyone.

The only one not seeing it sometimes is you. You are that sunshine, that warmth that you are looking for.
You can give that to yourself and then you can share it with others too.

You can be the observer.
Stay out of the story.
Trust the play.

You are the creator of your life, good and bad.
You can trust yourself and the universe.
Everything happens at the right time.

Life brings infinite creative opportunities.
You can create whatever you want.
You have that power.
You not having it, is the biggest illusion.

Ecstasy is our birthright.

We are here to thrive and enjoy life!

I allow myself to receive more.

What can you do to get your vibration higher?
What gets you most excited?

The sun sends you love every day, can you feel it?
That immense power and warmth.
The more you bathe in it,
the more you will feel it inside.
Time to shine and light up this world.

Feel that you are on the beach and
feel the sun on your skin.
Everything that is troubling you falls away.
And you just are.

The more I love myself, the more the world reflects that love back at me.

What makes you come alive the most?
Are you following your heart's desires?
What are you most passionate about?
How can you create that even more for yourself, for the people around you, and for the world?

What seeds are you planting???
Every day is a gift,
Start seeing it as one.
You are life itself.
What can you do today that will make you very happy?

You are a phoenix rising from the ashes
and becoming the most vibrant version of yourself.

You are a gift.
See the light you are emanating in yourself and around the world.

The more you are aligned with yourself and your purpose, the more you will radiate that out to everyone.

Know you are loved
and know you are love.

Life is an ongoing process of evolving and learning. It is okay that it is not always easy.
Sometimes it's a bumpy road.
During those times we need to breathe through it. Trust and know you will get out on the other side again.

If you have a dark night of the soul,
know it is before you get a new sense of freedom, more love, and more aliveness.
Like a phoenix rising from the ashes
and as a butterfly after being a caterpillar.

No more fake idols.
Be the star of your own movie.

Everybody that does not accept you as you are, reminds you to accept yourself as you are.

What if you could live in a place, where whenever you meet a person, it was the last time you would ever see them again?
Would you say or do things differently?
Would you still judge them or project unto them? Maybe you could see them in awe and be grateful for them in your life and be the most kind and loving you can be.

Feel as if the whole of existence is making love to you.

Can you see the beauty?
It is in everything.
But mostly in yourself.

Let the world hold you and nurture you.
Mother Earth is here for you.

You experience everything as you are.
You create your reality.
Create it with love.

You come from the love of all your ancestors.
Can you imagine how much love was necessary to create you?
Be grateful for all your elders.

I AM LOVE.
I AM FREE.
I AM ME.

I love you just as you are.
Love yourself just as you are.

I give thanks to so many reasons to celebrate every day.
So much love and joy, life is amazing.
It truly is.
I AM grateful to be alive.

I AM grateful to breathe every breath.
I love life and life loves me back more and more each day.
Your body is your biggest teacher,
start listening to it more.

When you silence your mind and become more still, you
will hear the whispers of your soul.

My life is deliciously joyous.

I love myself.
I heal myself.
I accept myself.
I AM myself.
I AM beautiful.
I AM celebrated.
I AM worthy of all the love in the world.
I AM free.
I AM me.
I AM myself.

I AM good as I AM.
I AM a sovereign human being.
I AM a god/goddess.
I AM all.
I AM nothing.
I AM amazing.
I AM you.
I AM one with all that is.

The more you trust yourself,
the more you trust the universe.

In the depth of who you are,
lie hidden treasures,
waiting for you to discover them.

Everything is always happening for the right reason, even
though you might find it out only later.

It's time to become the hero of your own story and to unleash your greatness into the world.

If your outside world does not bring you happiness, start aligning your inner world by going within. There you will find your happiness back.

We are the medicine,
we bring into the world.
Everybody has their own unique vibration
and together we are one big sacred symphony.
Everybody matters and is equally important.
We are all medicine men and women.
It is now the time to remember.
We are made for these times.

No fear, be here.

I AM grateful for all my ancestors.
Without them, I would not be here now.

We are the living prayers they spoke of.
Every step is sacred, every minute of every day.

Do you change because the universe forces you?
Or do you choose to change ahead of time while you hear
the whispers of the universe?

Do you realize that life is one big love song, especially for
you?

Just relax,
things are ok right now and will even be better.
Life is one big journey to yourself.

I live in heaven on earth
and all the right things come to me at the right time.

If you could see yourself as God sees you,
you would finally see how magnificently beautiful you are.

Stand in your own power
and everything around you will help you to shine even
more.
You can do more than you think.
Start believing in yourself even more.

We are here to show others the light,
so they can see it in themselves.

Let life be one big celebration.

You were never too much.
Keep rising, being you, and spreading your magic.

Look inside and know that the whole universe is inside of
you.

Hey there, yes you, just wanting to say:
You are awesome.
You are beautiful.

You are on the right path.
You can just relax and know, that the universe will take care of everything.

Look inside the mirror and fall in love with the person looking at you.
This is the love you have been searching for your whole life.

I AM love.
I AM truth.
I AM you.
I AM me.
We are all one.

It is time for humanity to rise
and become the powerful beings that we were always supposed to be.
Let's rise up and know the world is ours.

Love where you are now.
The place.
The relationship.
The job.
Because you are now in it, it is the right one.
Let go of any worry and relax in the now.
If it needs to change, that moment will come at the right time.

We came here to remember the old ways.
To connect again with ourselves and the earth.
Life is worthwhile and be grateful for every moment.
We are love
and still, we sometimes need reminders from the universe
to see and feel it.

I AM loved.
I AM awesome.
I AM amazing.
I AM beautiful.
I AM light.

I AM joy.
I AM love.
I AM abundance.
I AM blessed, we all are,
We just have to say it, feel it and believe it.

I AM worthy of all the beautiful things the universe
offers me.

The more I AM myself.
The more bliss I experience.

My heart is expanding every day
and I go where it leads me.

If you are not afraid.
You are invincible and free.

When you are in peace with the non-peace, you make
peace with all.

In the right time,
all the puzzle pieces will come together.

By expressing ourselves fully,
we become more ourselves.
And we inspire others to express themselves more as well.

Taking full responsibility,
gives us total acceptance and freedom over our reality

Everything is love expressing itself.

You are so loved.
You have no idea.
If so, you would never be lonely or sad.
All your guides, spirits, and angels are around you.
No need to worry.
Just let go
and let everything happen like it should happen.

Allow yourself to receive more love.
Allow yourself to receive it from the wind, the stars, the
moon, the sun, the trees, the plants, and the flowers.
Connect to nature and to Mother Earth.
And you will connect more to yourself.

Just be you.
And keep on shining.
Not everybody will see you.
If you like the person you are,
you are never alone and you will always be in the best
company.

Every time you come into a new version of yourself, you
will feel more free and more in love with yourself and life.

Everything is manifested for your highest good and the
highest good of all.
I am grateful for everything in my life,
because I know I choose everything myself, consciously or
unconsciously.

The more you are conscious the more you create it with open eyes.

You are worthy of all the love in the world.
You deserve to be fully loved for who you are.

You are such a gift to this world.
With every step on the earth, you create ripples of love wherever you are.

Paradise is within and where you are.
See it, feel it, and know it.

You are love incarnated and you don't need any confirmation to know you are.

Keep enjoying and shining your light no matter what is going on around you.

Create a blank sheet and from there start creating.
Know you are the master in creating yourself and your life.

Keep smiling,
it brings electric signals to the brain so you become even
happier.

Trust that whatever is happening is for the betterment of
all.
Keep trusting in the universe, that is you.

You are amazing, never doubt that.
You are supported by the whole universe and all the
beings in it.
The sun, animals, humans, everything is here for you.
Everything is love even sadness.
It has a purpose in your evolution.
You grow and you become stronger and there will be
more love.

You are here to be adored, to be loved as you love.

You are a visionary.
You are the energy of the new earth.
You breathe it.
You live it.
You are it.
Can you feel it?

You were always waiting for you.
To step into the real you.
The full you.
The most magnificent you.
The full potential you.

Life force ON.
Superpowers ON.
You are the master of your own universe.

I am on a journey
toward more fun, adventure, and excitement.
Life is one crazy adventure.

Can it get even better?
Yes! Says the universe.

Dancing

Life is one big dance.
Give it all you've got fully in,
no regrets, just surrendering
to this now moment.
You will never know how long it will last,
make it the best and have a blast!

Love grows,
even when you don't notice.
If a plant grows you also do not always see that it grows,
but you still know.

Patience is one of my biggest teachers.
Why can't I already have it all and now?
But then, what is more exciting: not knowing what will

come and maybe it's even better than ever expected or knowing everything?
Relax, it will all come at the right time.

Doubt can be a good thing.
If you did not have any doubt, you would not question. If you would not question, would you have found out what you know now?

Awesomeness is here!

Thank you universe for all of it!!!
I could not have done it without you.

Become the shining star of your own movie,
but also the director, writer, and the screen.
Accept that it is sometimes a romance, sometimes a drama, sometimes a horror movie, but there is always excitement to see the next part and there is nobody who

could play your role as magnificently as you can.

How could you forget who you are?
You are divine
You are love
You are the culmination of all the love of your ancestors.
You are all that you are.
You are whole and you are free.
And I know it and I hope you remember.
Just remember

Remember who you are.

There must be some kind of angel flapping her wings in another dimension to cheer me on.

We are the light that lights up this world.

New Earth

New earth is here.

You create it with every step you make.

Every breath you take.

Every thought you have.

Every word you spell.

Every act you do.

Let it all come from a place of love,

and it will become a place of love for all.

Lots of love to all of you co-creating heaven on earth
with me.

Without you, the world would be a different place.

Happy and honored to be here with you all.

Let's do this together!

Author Bio:

Janneke Hellebrekers, aka MissHellbreaker, comes from the Netherlands and has lived in different countries around the world for several years.

She offers yoga, meditation, coaching, energy healings, courses, dance, and workshops-both online and offline-to people worldwide. She is also very active on social media, with lots of videos, talks, and a podcast that spreads seeds of awakening. She helps others become more free-energetically, emotionally, mentally, physically, and financially. She is dedicated to a healthy lifestyle and self-growth.

She feels she has broken free from the matrix (system) and lives in paradise. She brightens up the world with her joy, love, and happiness and helps people find that within themselves too.

Misshellbreaker.com

www.ingramcontent.com/pod-product-compliance
Lightning Source LLC
Chambersburg PA
CBHW051557120626
46551CB00013B/1560